Table of Contents

Mindset, Goal Setting & Engagement
For Life & Work

Cultivating
SOFT
SKILLS

Christina DeMara

Author and Creator of Meaningful Leadership
& Early Life Leadership in Children

Chapter 1
Cultivating Soft Skills

Every skill you acquire doubles your odds of success.
- Scott Adams

What are soft skills?

Soft Skills: These are also known as interpersonal skills or people skills. Soft skills combine how we interact with others, personality traits, communication style, and social cues.

Why are soft skills important?

Soft skills are critical in today's workplace and are viewed as an investment. Soft skills set people apart. Those who value and implement soft skills are recognized as essential employees rather than merely good employees. In a competitive world of job seeking, college applications, and job promotions, soft skills can make all the difference in an interview. Soft skills make a huge difference between blending in and being unforgettable. *Why?* Because even though some soft skills may be practical or common sense, it is difficult to get people to apply these soft skills consistently and with a glad heart. Organizations seek individuals who value and want to engage in self-development, grow into leaders, and are consistently great. Those who prioritize soft skills interact more effectively with customers and colleagues. Employers value soft skills because they know soft skills are the foundational framework for thriving teams and happy people.

Soft skills are interpersonal qualities, also known as people skills and personal attributes. Business executives consider soft skills a vital attribute in job applicants. Therefore, employers want new employees to have strong soft skills. Those who possess strong soft skills such as effective communication, getting along well with their coworkers, embracing teamwork, taking initiative, possessing a high work ethic, and portraying professionalism, which are respected attributes (Robles, 2012).

Why are soft skills necessary in life and work?

Did you know soft skills are critical in today's workplace and life? I chose to write this book from the perspective of life and work because I believe they overlap. If we are not happy at home, it trickles into our work. If we are not satisfied at work, it trickles into our personal life. We need soft skills for both life and career because we are continually growing and maintaining our relationships with others. Life looks different for everyone. We all are at different places in life, and we all travel down different paths, but the one thing that we have in common is that we all want to live a good life. A peaceful life. A productive life. A successful life. That is why soft skills are so critical.

Work may look like making dinner for your family or you may be in a small office. On the other hand, you may work in a large building with a bunch of people. You may be self-employed and have the luxury to work from home in your pajamas. Nevertheless, we need to build our interpersonal skills to be the best possible version of ourselves every day.

1. Willingness to Learn

Definition: A deep desire to acquire new knowledge and develop one-self to be better.

How do I cultivate a willingness to learn?

Cultivating the willingness to learn is not easy because when we finish school or training, there is a sense of completion as in "I'm done." However, we are never done learning. Therefore, we must look at everyone who crosses our path as teachers and every situation as a learning or teachable moment.

Changing My Mindset: The willingness to learn comes from within. I have been blessed to work with some of the best professionals around, because of that, people frequently assume that my job is always easy. I often get comments like, "Those people work with you? They are amazing at what they do. Your job must be easy." Yes, I have led amazing people, and because of that, I had to open my mind to be willing to learn from them, so they could respect me and be willing to learn from me. The willingness to learn comes from mutual respect for one another. Willingness to learn always means, "I want to pay attention in trainings I want to learn. I want to be better." If we refuse to learn, we will stop growing.

Reflection: Willingness to Learn

1. I want to learn more about…

2. Learning is difficult because…

3. I am willing to learn because…

4. Willingness to learn looks like…

2. Deep Discussions

Definition: A serious conversation where one says, "Can we talk?" and asks questions or discloses something important, such as a safety or human resource issue.

How do I cultivate "Deep Discussions"?

Understanding how to communicate effectively is critical to our personal and professional success. Common communication snags include over speaking, lecturing, complaining, and talking down to others. Basic communication skills include "ask☒tell☒ask," "tell me more," and responding empathetically (Back, Arnold, Baile, Tulsky, & Fryer☒ Edwards, 2005).

When approaching complex communication tasks, such as giving bad news or criticism, there is no way to predict how the person receiving the information will react, no matter how strong your relationship.

Changing My Mindset: Deep discussions are never easy, but we have to communicate every day to make communication easier. Be intentional about participating in meetings and group discussions. Take opportunities to team build and establish strong relationships with the people in your life. When you need to have a deep discussion with them, the person receiving the information will listen and respect what you communicate. The deep discussion mindset should be "I want the person listening to me to be better." Deep discussions are necessary and should always offer suggestions for resolution, be calm, factual, and respectful.

Reflection: Deep Discussions

Deep discussions are difficult because...

Deep discussions look like...

Deep discussions have taught me...

Deep discussions are important because...

3. Team-Oriented

Definition: A mindset that believes participating in a team of two or more people, who work together enthusiastically toward a common and valued goal /purpose/objective is effective for all stakeholders.

How do I cultivate a team-oriented mindset?

Your team is only as good as your leader. Many people will tell you they are more efficient if they work alone. This might be due to a bad experience or personality. Despite your preference, working together with others is something we cannot escape, so embrace it. Establishing a solid team foundation contributes to team effectiveness, a more significant level of collective expertise, teaches leadership, distributes responsibilities, results in fewer misunderstandings when decision making, and achieves a higher goal performance (Zaccaro, Rittman, & Marks, 2001).

Changing My Mindset: The failure to change your mindset, limits the growth and development of people and organizations because whether we want to admit it or not, we learn from one another. Embrace a team-oriented mindset by journaling self-critiques of what went right and wrong in team meetings. Avoid procrastination when planning for group activities, get to know your members and their strengths, accept feedback and ideas from others, and focus on tasks at hand. If you are seriously team-oriented, others will follow.

Reflection: Team-Oriented Mindset

A team-oriented mindset is difficult because...

A team-oriented mindset looks like...

Working within a team has taught me...

A team-oriented mindset is important because...

4. Take Initiative

Definition: To be internally prompted to take action to do something good without being asked to.

How do I cultivate "taking initiative?"

Taking the initiative is challenging because we have so much to do, and to take on more tasks within the same amount of time is difficult. In addition, when we are busy trying to finish our work and accomplish personal goals, making it hard to take initiative. However, you can take initiative by leaving things better than you found them, being proactive and using and improving systems, procedures, and policies.

Changing My Mindset:

Taking initiative is an intentional mindset to do things for others without having them ask. The mindset must be that taking initiative is as important as the rest of my life and work. If we intentionally take the time to do things without being asked, that says a lot about our character and goes a long way toward impressing others. I would go as far as to set an alarm on my phone as a reminder or even journal one thing each day I accomplished without being requested. In a fast-paced world, where there is little time to take initiative, we must set a daily or weekly reminder. These small acts will make you feel happy and more accomplished.

Reflection: Taking Initiative

A "taking the initiative" mindset is difficult because...

A "taking the initiative" mindset looks like...

"Taking the initiative" has taught me...

A "taking the initiative" mindset is important because...

"Taking the initiative" makes me feel...

5. Conflict Resolution

Definition: An act of resolving conflict through mutual agreement or meeting someone halfway.

How do I cultivate conflict resolution?

When it comes to conflict, there are only two sides. You are either part of the problem or part of the solution. It is not about being right or wrong. To move forward from a conflict, one must see things from this perspective.

Changing My Mindset: The most challenging thing about conflict is that emotions run high. Very quickly, things turn into a power struggle and can become personal. Most of the time, it was something small that could have been resolved promptly, but maybe we were too intimidated to speak up, we were not honest about our feelings, or perhaps, we just didn't like the other person.

Conflict can be one of the most dangerous of all soft skills. However, the key word is resolution. We must change our mindset to believe that there is always a resolution in every conflict. There is always a middle ground. There is always room for more leaders and more ideas. Conflict can be resolved with a little bit of time, patience, and communication. We will see less conflict and more positive energy if we change our mindset.

Reflection: Conflict Resolution

Conflict resolution is difficult because...

A conflict resolution mindset looks like...

Conflict resolution has taught me...

A conflict resolution mindset is important because...

When I strive to use conflict resolution, it makes me feel...

10 Behaviors People Do That Cause Conflict

1. Refuses to work with another "certain" team member.

2. Always making negative comments.

3. Constantly telling jokes and gets people off track.

4. Whispering to others or starting side conversations during discussions.

5. Getting upset when his/her recommendations are not accepted.

6. Being late.

7. Not being engaged or helping.

8. Leaving before the job/work is done.

9. Dominating the conversation/discussion.

10. Taking over and delegates.

6. Crisis Management

Definition: A sequence of actions taken, performed by an organization to prepare for, or prevent, an adverse event, disruption of business operations, or to mitigate a safety threat.

How do I cultivate crisis management?

When we create systems (policies and procedures), we create awareness. Some may think it is somewhat strange to include crisis management as a soft skill, but I think it is important because times are changing. We have an influx of people suffering from depression and suicidal thoughts. We are connected to a diverse population who may have medical conditions or a disability. Things may be confidential in the workplace, so you cannot expect human resources to disclose other people's information to you. It is important to be aware and recognize when those around us are not their normal selves.

Changing My Mindset: We must change our mindset to be aware of crisis issues. Asking for help is not a weakness. So many people struggle alone. The philosophy we need to cultivate is if we see anyone or anything that does not look right; we must get that person help right away. This might happen when you overhear a conversation; perhaps you hear someone talking on the phone, saying they are so tired and do not want to live anymore. Or maybe you see somebody who looks pale and sweats a lot. We are not medical professionals. It is not our place to say that person is sick or okay. However, offer help and get help if needed. "Hey friend, are you okay?" goes a long way. Connect with your crisis leader if you have questions about organizational protocols.

Reflection: Crisis Management

Crisis management is difficult because...

A crisis management mindset looks like...

Crisis management has taught me...

Cultivating a crisis management mindset is important because...

When using crisis management, it makes me feel...

10 Crises You Needs to Plan For

1   Substance Abuse

2   Suicide

3   Medical

4   Someone with a weapon

5   Mental Health & Depression

6   Natural Disaster

7   Rumors & Hostility

8   Technology Outages

9   Organizational Shut Down

10   Strike

7. Strengths & Weakness

Definition: Strengths and weaknesses are simply what a person can do really well and what a person either cannot do or needs more practice doing.

How do I cultivate my strengths and improve on my weaknesses?

Cultivating your strengths and improving on weaknesses comes from understanding who you are in life and at work. It requires a person to be honest about their skill levels and talents.

Changing My Mindset: When I ask people what their strengths and weaknesses are, 99 percent of the time, I get strange faces. People are taken back. Some faces look confused, and some faces look defensive. Some people can go on and on and on about their strengths; however, when it comes to their weaknesses, they have a very difficult time assessing them. The mindset that we need to have when it comes to our strengths and weaknesses is that our strengths are just as important as our weaknesses. If we do not know our weaknesses, how will we grow? How can we be intentional about our learning? We must change the mindset that weaknesses are a bad thing. Weaknesses are not bad. We all have them. I want to encourage you to think about who you are and how others perceive you in life and work.

Reflection: Strengths & Weaknesses

Cultivating "strengths and weaknesses" is difficult because...

Cultivating a mindset that values "strengths and weaknesses" looks like...

Cultivating strengths and improving on weaknesses has taught me...

Knowing your "strengths and weaknesses" is important because...

When I know my "strengths and weaknesses", it makes me feel...

8. Time Management

Definition: The process of organizing and planning how to divide your time between specific activities. Good time management enables you to work smarter – not harder – so that you get more done in less time, even when time is tight and pressures are high. Failing to manage your time damages your effectiveness and causes stress.

How do I cultivate time management?

To cultivate time management, we must know what works for us and what holds us back from finishing tasks.

Changing My Mindset: Often, when people hear the word time management, they feel overwhelmed, and some have even told me they feel anxious. We need to change our mindset from hurry up, the clock is ticking, to these are the strategies that work well for me, and this is how I get the most done. When we reflect and get to know ourselves on what works and doesn't work, we can get more done. Some people use calendars, some use reminders on their phones, some like to get things done as fast as possible, but others try to pace themselves. Some people feel like they get more done alone, and others accomplish more by delegating to one another. Reflect on what works best for you, and remember to complete each task with integrity.

Reflection: Time Management

Time management is difficult because...

Cultivating a mindset that values time management looks like...

Cultivating time management has taught me...

Time management is important because...

When I know my strengths and weakness, it makes me feel...

9. Giving Compliments

Definition: Giving a compliment is the act of giving someone positive praise or appreciation.

How do I cultivate "giving compliments?"

We cultivate giving compliments by setting a personal goal of giving one compliment a week, then moving on to one compliment a day. There is a saying that people will forget what you say, but they will never forget how you make them feel. Giving people compliments will help build trust, respect, and appreciation at work and in life.

Changing My Mindset: When we think about giving compliments, there is a stereotype of noticing a nice haircut or a nice tie. There are many different types of feedback we can provide people to critique their performance, but we must even out criticism with compliments. Don't only fill people with constructive criticism. You must change your mindset to one that says we are here to build people up and help them grow, not micromanage them, and not put them down. Giving compliments goes a long way. It may even increase work environment satisfaction.

Reflection: Compliments

"Giving compliments" is difficult because...

Cultivating a mindset that values "giving compliments" looks like...

"Giving compliments" has taught me...

"Giving compliments" is important because...

"Giving compliments" makes me feel...

10. Accepting Constructive Criticism

Definition: The process of receiving valid and well-reasoned opinions on how one can improve.

How do I cultivate "accepting constructive criticism?"

To accept constructive criticism first, one must respect the person giving the criticism. If there is no trust and respect between the two exchanging opinions for improvement, one may take things personally and become defensive.

Changing My Mindset: Three things need to change in our mindset when accepting criticism. First, we cannot take things personally. Second, we must believe and trust that the person giving us the criticism wants us to be better. Third, we must be positive and think this is an opportunity to grow and become better.

Reflection: Acceptance of Constructive Criticism

Accepting constructive criticism is difficult because...

Accepting constructive criticism looks like...

Accepting constructive criticism has taught me...

Accepting constructive criticism is important because...

Accepting constructive criticism makes me feel...

11. Journaling

Definition: Journaling is a process where we reflect and write notes inside a diary, journal, or spiral notebook. Everybody's journaling looks different, but each provides a place for someone to document a life journey or their emotions.

How do I cultivate journaling?

Journaling looks different for everyone. It may happen in a notebook or even on a computer document to preserve one's privacy. The key is just to write and not worry about spelling and grammar but to spill all your emotions and ideas out.

Changing My Mindset: Journaling helps with emotional and mental well-being. Journaling may help relieve stress and helps us keep a positive state of mind. Journaling is not just for women—journaling is for everyone. We must change our mindset. Journaling increases productivity, emotional well-being, creativity and helps build a buffer between negative thoughts and ideas. If someone struggles with stress and depression, journaling may help them gain control of their emotions and ideas. This is also a great way to document your innovative ideas and look back at them later for inspiration.

Reflection: Journaling

Journaling is difficult because...

Journaling looks like...

Journaling has taught me...

Journaling is important because…

Journaling makes me feel...

12. Thinking with the End in Mind

Definition: Thinking with the end in mind means you begin each day or project with a clear vision of where you want to be at the end of your destination.

How do I cultivate "thinking with the end in mind?"

Cultivating the end in mind sounds easier said than done. We develop the best outcome for a project or campaign within a group or committee. This is true even for a family trip. The best way to start cultivating your vision is to plan for the end.

Changing My Mindset:

It is always important to think about the end first when starting a project. What is the end goal? What is the final objective? Starting backwards sounds like an odd thing, but we are more successful when we change our mindset to have a clear direction.

Reflection: "Thinking with the end in mind."

Cultivating "thinking with the end in mind" is difficult because...

Cultivating a mindset that values "thinking with the end in mind" looks like...

Cultivating "thinking with the end in mind" has taught me...

"Thinking with the end in mind" is important because...

When I am "thinking with the end in mind," it makes me feel...

13. Do the Right Thing
(Even When No One is Looking)

Definition: The ethical responsibility to make decisions in the best interest of everyone around us.

How do I cultivate "do the right thing?"

Doing the right thing is very difficult to teach or explain because it may look different to each person. We must make decisions based on organizational policy and the people's best interests at work and in our lives.

Changing My Mindset: Doing the right thing is difficult sometimes. If you should not park there, do not park there. If you know you need to do something, do it. We need to move away from the mindset of doing what is easy and convenient. We need to do what is right for everyone and what is in the people's best interest in our life and at work. We must change our mindset and do the right thing. People take notice and follow. They will trust and respect you. Doors will start to open because people feel like they can trust each other and that each of us will do the right thing. When we have a reputation for doing the right thing, we become more successful in life and work.

Reflection: "Doing the Right Thing"

"Doing the right thing" is difficult because...

"Doing the right thing" looks like...

"Doing the right thing" has taught me...

"Doing the right thing" is important because…

"Doing the right thing" makes me feel...

14. Creativity

Definition: Creativity is when we use our childlike instincts and imagination to think outside the box. To create something abstract or something extraordinary.

How do I cultivate creativity?

Everybody cultivates creativity differently. I often say that I have my best ideas in the shower. When I am in the shower, I am decompressing and relaxing. I am clearing my mind to create room for new ideas. For some people, it may be journaling or doing something creative such as painting or sketching. For others, this process may be more formal such as a brainstorming session with their team members at work.

Changing My Mindset:

Changing our mindset to be more creative will look different for everyone. There are four things I like to do to be creative: (1) I like to wake up early and journal, (2) I try new things and go to new places such as museums, art exhibits, or concerts, (3) I like to research to see what is out there on the internet, (4) I participate in brainstorming sessions with my team. I like to use a big whiteboard with dry markers to illustrate our ideas. Sometimes, I use sticky notes to move ideas and core concepts around.

Reflection: Creativity

Creativity is difficult because…

Creativity looks like…

Creativity has taught me…

Creativity is important because...

Creativity makes me feel…

15. Adaptability

Definition: Adaptability is being able to adjust to changes in our life without feeling overwhelmed or anxious.

How do I cultivate adaptability?

Cultivating adaptability starts with having an open mind and truly believing that everything is constantly changing. We also need to be aware of our emotional responses to change, and be ready to shift our behavior.

Changing My Mindset:

Accepting that everything is constantly changing.

Understanding that with technology, things change quickly.

When change occurs at work or home, see it in a positive light and welcome the new opportunity.

Reflection: Adaptability

Adaptability is difficult because...

Adaptability looks like...

Adaptability has taught me...

Adaptability is important because...

Adaptability makes me feel...

16. Work Well Under Pressure

Definition: What is the ability to work well under pressure? This relates to how you respond when put under pressure. In a work context, pressure can be defined as the stress or urgency of matters requiring attention, the burden of physical or mental distress, and the constraint of circumstances.

How do I cultivate working well under pressure?

Slow down. When you face a stressful situation and are working under pressure, you may feel the urge to speed up your thinking and actions.

Clear expectations.

Break down a project to "bite-size" tasks and delegate.

Go back to the basics.

Forget the juggle struggle — Prioritize.

Communicate effectively.

Changing My Mindset:

Often, there is so much going on we start to feel pressured and overwhelmed. There are not enough hours in the day, and we cannot clone ourselves. This requires a mindset change. There are three things we need to tell ourselves in those moments: (1) I am giving my best. (2) It will get done. (3) Doing things right rather than fast is best.

Reflection: "Work Well Under Pressure"

"Working Well Under Pressure" is difficult because...

"Working Well Under Pressure" looks like...

"Working Well Under Pressure" has taught me...

"Working Well Under Pressure" is important because...

"Working Well Under Pressure" makes me feel...

17. Self-motivation

Definition: To inspire oneself to take charge or continue a task without another's prodding, motivation, or supervision.

How do I cultivate self-motivation?

The most important thing you can do to ignite the self-motivation spark is to surround yourself around other people who are self-motivated. Unmotivated people will only bring you down. Surround yourself with go-getters, shakers, and movers.

Changing My Mindset:

High-level discussions will keep you self-motivated by discussing concepts and sharing ideas.

Find an accountability partner for something you need to finish.

Set goals within a reasonable time frame.

When encountering obstacles, remember it is only temporary. Obstacles are not permanent. You are not defeated. Keep going.

Keep learning.

Reflection: Self-Motivation

Self-motivation is difficult because…

Self-motivation looks like…

Self-motivation has taught me…

Self-motivation is important because...

Self-motivation makes me feel…

18. Body Language

Definition: To communicate through nonverbal cues, through postures, gestures, facial expressions.

How do I cultivate the right body language?

Awareness and intentionality can help you send the correct body language message to other people.

Changing My Mindset:

The mindset change for body language is realizing and valuing our bodies as a tool for life and work. For example, we could nod our head when people speak, so they know that we are paying attention. Welcoming customers with a smile or simply putting our arms around a loved one when they are talking to us lets them know we feel love and compassion for them.

Reflection: Body Language

Displaying the right "body language" is difficult because...

Displaying the right "body language" looks like...

Displaying the right "body language" has taught me...

Displaying the right "body language" is important because...

Displaying the right "body language" makes me feel...

The 10 Most Common Body Languages

1. Smile

2. Make eye contact

3. Nod to acknowledge the speaker

4. Firm handshake (Pre-covid)

5. Nod or elbow bump (post-covid)

6. Upright and open posture when sitting

7. Try not to cross your arms

8. Relax and try not to fidget

9. Proximity

10. Vocal Tone

19. Friendliness

Definition: Friendliness is a quality of openness and warmth that makes us feel welcome and comfortable.

How do I cultivate friendliness?

Smile

Welcome or talk to people.

Give a positive compliment.

Call people by their name.

Be helpful.

Changing My Mindset:

We really need to believe that being friendly is important. Being friendly sounds easy, but one of the things I hear people tell me is how they were poorly treated in a restaurant or public place. However, being friendly is contagious. When one person is friendly, it is easy to be friendly also. So let us change our mindset to, "I want to be treated friendly so, I'm going to treat others friendly too."

Reflection: Friendliness

Being friendly is difficult because...

Being friendly looks like...

Being friendly has taught me...

Being friendly is important because…

Being friendly makes me feel...

20. Resourceful

Definition: Resourceful is when you use what you already have to fix a problem.

How do I cultivate being resourceful?

Always know what resources are available in life and at work. When problem solving or creating an event, set a goal to always use what is available first. This helps save time and money.

Changing My Mindset: Changing your mindset to being resourceful is a good thing. Being resourceful can save time and money.

Ask others what they need to do their job before ordering or buying anything.

When planning, include different people to help pitch in or donate.

Use what we already have in front of us.

Utilize free technology and apps.

When we have a need or idea, Google it. What are other people doing? Learn from their experience.

Reflection: Resourceful

Being resourceful is difficult because...

Being resourceful looks like...

Being resourceful has taught me...

Being resourceful is important because...

Being resourceful makes me feel...

21. Research Skills

Definition: The ability to search for information to learn and make things better or to make a decision.

How do I cultivate research skills?

Growing your research skills is very easy, and some of you may have already done so. Back in the day, research happened at the library through periodical articles. Today, we have research at the tip of our fingers, starting with a good internet search.

Changing My Mindset:

Changing our mindset to growing research skills is important. Everything we do requires research, including our life and work decisions. Otherwise, we are pinning the tail on the donkey with a blindfold on.

Reflection: Research Skills

Research is difficult because...

Research looks like...

Research has taught me...

Research is important because...

Research makes me feel...

10 Things You Need to Research for a Better Life

1 Family / Health / Economic Trends

2 How to Get out of Debt

3 Healthy Recipes

4 Family Activities

5 Finding the Importance of Something

6 Creativity

7 Discovering Your Life's Purpose

8 Stress Relievers

9 Top Rated Books

10 Super Foods

*Consult your doctor before making any health changes.

10 Things You Need to Research for Work

1   Use technology such as apps and search engines like Google Scholar and Google Trends.

2   All social media platforms

3   Search Engine Optimization

4   Become more familiar with handling data

5   Algorithm Design

6   Data Presentation

7   Mobile Development

8   Networking through social media

9   Marketing Campaign Management

10   Virtualization

22. Attention to Detail

Definition: Attention to detail is a characteristic of the view of tasks and refers to meticulousness, precision, and accuracy.

How do I cultivate Attention to Detail?

If paying attention to detail is difficult, start small. If this is a weakness area, find a go-to person who can double-check things for you and offer to double-check their things in return.

Changing My Mindset:

Details can be very small things like numbers in a budget or sending off a memo. However, you are never too qualified not to have someone double-check your work because there are too many things going on, and our minds are in other places sometimes.

Reflection: Attention to Detail

Attention to detail is difficult because...

Attention to detail looks like...

Attention to detail has taught me...

Attention to detail is important because…

Attention to detail makes me feel...

23. Know Your Superpower

Definition: The skill, strength, or ability, which makes you succeed in life. It is what enables you to outperform others.

How do I cultivate my Superpower?

Knowing our superpower is a great way to help others and stay self-motivated. This starts with understanding our strengths, passions, and maybe even acknowledging a huge hurdle that we overcame.

Changing My Mindset: Do not be self-defeated. We all have a super-power. In addition, do not be overly confident. We all have weaknesses, but a superpower is a strength that helps other people. Perhaps you are a great problem solver, motivator, or peacemaker. Alternatively, maybe you love to read, have a good eye for grammar, and do not mind checking everybody's memos. How can you help others with your su-perpower?

Reflection: Your Superpower

Knowing my superpower is difficult because...

Knowing my superpower looks like...

Knowing my superpower has taught me...

Knowing my superpower is important because...

Knowing my superpower makes me feel...

24. Be Teachable

Definition: The capability of being taught and the willingness to learn without conflict.

How do I cultivate being teachable?

This starts by displaying three things: an open mind, a humble heart, and the willingness to grow and learn more.

Changing My Mindset: It does not matter how high we are on the totem pole, how long we have been in our profession, or how many certifications we have. When we stop learning, we stop growing. There is no way around it. In today's society, technology is moving lightning fast. We must be able to learn to help our organizations grow. In addition, we should also take time to learn from the people in our life. I know my teenage daughter helps me with technology issues.

Reflection: Teachable

Being teachable is difficult because...

Being teachable looks like...

Being teachable has taught me...

Being teachable is important because...

Being teachable makes me feel...

25. Phone Etiquette

Definition: Proper manners for representing yourself or your business to others over the phone.

How do I cultivate Phone Etiquette?

Phone etiquette sounds very simple, but it is hard to believe how many times I have witnessed or experienced somebody answering the phone, sounding like they really hate their job. How do people perceive us when we answer the phone?

Changing My Mindset:

We must change our mindset to believe that phone etiquette is important. Sometimes, it's the first impression for a client or a customer that helps or hurts us. We want everybody's experience to be top-notch, every time. We must be intentional in how we want others to perceive us. Every time we pick up the phone, whether it is a client, another staff member, a loved one, or a relative, we make the caller feel welcomed. I can tell right away what kind of day somebody is having by the way they answer the phone.

Reflection: Phone Etiquette

Phone etiquette is difficult because...

Phone etiquette looks like...

Learning about phone etiquette has taught me...

Phone etiquette is important because…

Strong phone etiquette makes me feel...

10 Ways to Have Good Phone Etiquette

1   Answer the call within three rings.

2   Use appropriate language.

3   Immediately introduce yourself.

    "Hello, my name is _____. How can I help you today?"

4   Check for and reply to voicemails.

5   Stay cheerful.

6   Speak clearly.

7   Ask before putting someone on hold or transferring a call.

    "Is it okay if I put you on hold for a minute, so I can better help you?"

8   Only use speakerphone when necessary. (It is choppy or hard to ear.)

9   Be honest if you do not know the answer.

10   Be aware of your volume.

    Actively listen and take notes. (Add date and time)

26. Positive Attitude

Definition: The attention to the positive things in life rather than the negative.

How do I cultivate a Positive Attitude?

Attitude is everything. There is so much going on in life, good and bad, but it is a matter of perception. We must choose to see the good in people, situations, and our place in life.

Changing My Mindset: Some people think positive attitudes are over-rated. I would argue that. Sometimes, we can get frustrated with our workplace, group projects, and even the family's attitude in a vehicle for hours at a time on a family trip. In those situations, we can either moan and groan, make faces, roll eyes; or we can be positive and treat others the way we want to be treated. Do not be part of the problem, be part of the solution instead. We must set the example. If things are to get better, we must set the tone and the expectation for the others on our team. In your personal life, cherish your time with loved ones and enjoy it. Your attitude is a choice.

Reflection: Positive Attitude

Cultivating a positive attitude is difficult because...

A positive attitude looks like...

A positive attitude taught me...

A positive attitude is important because...

A positive attitude makes me feel...

27. Setting Boundaries

Definition: A limit or space between you and another person.

How do I cultivate Setting Boundaries?

Developing the need to set boundaries takes courage because nobody wants to be the bad guy. Boundaries start with clear and honest communication. You can even explain your limitations. I had an assistant that told me from day one, "I will help you organize, but I will not help you clean. I hate cleaning for others because I was the only girl when I was little. I had to clean, but my brothers didn't." I totally respected that response. However, if we are not honest about how we feel, those boundaries are not clear.

Changing My Mindset: Setting boundaries has a negative connotation. Establishing boundaries is a healthy thing. We must set boundaries so people know what is okay and what is not.

Reflection: Setting Boundaries

Setting boundaries is difficult because...

Setting boundaries looks like...

Setting boundaries has taught me...

Setting boundaries is important because…

Setting boundaries makes me feel...

28. Accepting "No"

Definition: To accept rejection in a non-personal way that does not evoke anger or sadness.

How do I cultivate Accepting "No"?

Make eye contact with the other person.

Nod and say, "Okay."

Peacefully ask for a reason if you really do not understand the no.

Changing My Mindset:

The biggest thing with 'Accepting no" is knowing it's not personal in your mind. Although, some may argue that it is personal because of thoughts like "I know she doesn't like me." There may be many things going on in the background you don't know about, such as budgeting, organizational changes, or restructuring. From a personal perspective, I believe accepting no is only temporary. If you want a yes, work at it. Make changes in your life to turn that "no" into a yes!

Reflection: Accepting "No"

Accepting "No" is difficult because...

Accepting "No" looks like...

Accepting "No" has taught me...

Accepting "No" is important because...

Accepting "No" makes me feel...

29. Respect Everyone and Everything

Definition: To show high or special regard for differences.

How do I cultivate "Respect Everyone and Everything"?

Treat people and objects the way you would like to be treated.

Approach people and objects with kindness, courteousness, and politeness.

Changing My Mindset:

So many times, we see messy public bathrooms, disrespected copy machines, or people working and living together who don't like each other. We need to shift our minds. Treat people the way you want to be treated, and treat that copy machine as if it was your own. Sometimes, I see people making a mess in a Walmart bathroom, and sometimes, I see people wash their hands, grab a paper towel, and dry and wipe the sink or countertop down. Who do you want to be?

Reflection: Respect Everyone and Everything

"Respecting everyone and everything" is difficult because…

"Respecting everyone and everything" looks like…

"Respecting everyone and everything" has taught me…

"Respecting everyone and everything" is important because

"Respecting everyone and everything" makes me feel.

30. Don't Take Things Personally

Definition: To be offended or upset by what someone said. To feel personally attacked by words or actions.

How do I cultivate "Don't Take Things Personally"?

Don't jump to conclusions.

Criticism helps us grow.

Let things go. Tomorrow is a new day.

Take the high road, and don't react.

Changing My Mindset:

Remember that everyone is fighting a personal battle. When we take things personally, it really has nothing to do with us most of the time. When we receive or hear criticism in our professional life, we should strive not to feel hurt or shamed. We need feedback so we can be better.

Reflection: "Don't Take Things Personally"

"Don't Take Things Personally" is difficult because...

"Don't Take Things Personally" looks like...

"Don't Take Things Personally" has taught me...

"Don't Take Things Personally" is important because...

"Don't Take Things Personally" makes me feel...

31. Pay It Forward

Definition: When someone does something for you, you pass it on to another person instead of paying that person back directly.

How do I cultivate "Pay It Forward"?

Hold the door open for the person behind you.

Introduce yourself. Make new colleagues, classmates, etc. feel welcome.

Listen intently to people's stories without trying to fix everything.

Donate blood or clothing in your community.

Volunteer to be a helping hand.

Inspire others online via social media by liking and sharing a post.

Changing My Mindset:

Paying it forward doesn't always have to be buying the coffee or order behind you. Not all people have the money to do that, but helping a new employee, giving a compliment, or volunteering to help on a project goes a long way.

Refection: Pay It Forward

1. *"Paying it Forward" looks like....*

2. *"Paying it Forward" feels like...*

3. *"Paying it Forward" taught me...*

4. *"Paying it Forward" is important because...*

5. *"Paying it Forward" make me feel...*

32. Treat Everyone the Way You Want to Be Treated

Definition: If you want to be treated kindly, treat others kindly, and then they shall treat you kindly. It also means that if you mistreat other people, they will mistreat you.

How do I cultivate
"Treat Everyone the Way You Want to Be Treated"?

Forgive those who have hurt or overlooked you.

Treat everyone with kindness.

Help those who need you.

Don't judge people.

Treat everyone with dignity.

Don't try to make yourself look good by making someone else look small.

Never look down on someone unless you are helping them up.

Appreciate those who have supported you.

Changing My Mindset:

You have to believe that if you treat people the way you want to be treated, (1) it's the right thing to do, (2) you will be better for it, and (3) karma will be good to you.

Refection: Treat Everyone the Way You Want to Be Treated

Treat Everyone the Way You Want to Be Treated is difficult because…

Treat Everyone the Way You Want to Be Treated looks like…

Treat Everyone the Way You Want to Be Treated had taught me…

Treat Everyone the Way You Want to Be Treated is important because…

Treat Everyone the Way You Want to Be Treated makes me feel…

33. Ask Questions

Definition: To ask questions when you are unsure, don't know, or are curious.

How do I cultivate the skill of asking questions?

Write your questions down.

If you need help, who cares? Do not be embarrassed. People naturally want to help.

There are people who probably have the same question.

Assuming or guessing will get you in trouble.

Changing My Mindset:

Sometimes, we feel shame when we ask questions. But there is nothing wrong with wanting to do things right or learn more. If asking questions gives you anxiety, write your questions down and meet with that person at a later time.

Refection: Ask Questions

Asking Questions is difficult because...

Asking Questions looks like...

Asking Questions has taught me...

Asking Questions important because...

Asking Questions makes me feel...

34. Only Complain if You Have a Solution

Definition: Only Complain if You Have a Solution (A blunt statement with no definition.)

How do I cultivate "Only Complain if You Have a Solution?"

If you are upset or feel the need to complain:

Write your complaint down.

Instead of complaining, ask questions.

Think about how to solve the problem before you complain.

Changing My Mindset:

Complaining or giving criticism without a solution can hurt the morale and energy of a meeting. There is no problem with asking questions or giving recommendations, but you need to do so with professionalism and tact.

Refection: Only Complain if You Have a Solution

"Only Complain if You Have a Solution" is difficult because…

"Only Complain if You Have a Solution" looks like…

"Only Complain if You Have a Solution" has taught me…

"Only Complain if You Have a Solution" is important because…

"Only Complain if You Have a Solution" makes me feel…

Chapter 2
Goal Setting

"By recording your dreams and goals on paper, you set in motion the process of becoming the person you most want to be. Put your future in good hands—your own."

—Mark Victor Hansen

Why is Goal Setting Important?

Goals are important because we are playing pin the tail on the donkey without them! We have no direction. Goals create action, direction, accountability, and inspire growth.

10 Reasons Why Goal Setting is Important?

1   Goals Create Accountability for Oneself

2   Goals Create Focus

3   Goals Create Timeline and Time Management

4   Goals Create Purpose

5   Goals Create the Desire to Learn and Grow

6   Goals Create Manageable Steps Toward a Bigger Goal

7   Goals Create a Boost of Self-Confidence

8   Goals Create the Need for Collaboration and Team Work

9   Goals Create a Clear Path

10   Goals Create Self Development and Growth

What does research say about goal setting?

1. When confronted with task goals, people automatically use the knowledge and skills they have already acquired that is relevant to goal attainment. For example, if the goal involves cutting logs, loggers use their knowledge of logging without the need for additional conscious planning in their choice to exert effort and persist until the goal is attained (Latham & Kinne, 1974).

2. People draw from a list of skills they have used previously in related contexts and apply them to the present situation. For example, Latham and Baldes (1975) found that truck drivers who were assigned the goal of increasing the weight of their truckloads made modifications to their trucks so that they could better estimate truck weight before driving to the weighing station (American Psychologist, 2002).

3. If the task for which a goal is assigned is new to people, they will deliberate planning to develop strategies that will enable them to attain their goals (Smith, Locke, & Barry, 1990).

4. People with high self-efficacy are more likely to develop effective goal strategies than those with low self-efficacy (Latham, Winters, & Locke, 1994; Wood & Bandura, 1989).

5. When people are confronted with a complex task, urging them to do their best sometimes leads to better strategies (Earley, Connolly, & Ekegren, 1989).

6. When people are trained in the proper strategies, those given specific high-performance goals are more likely to use those strategies than those given other goals; hence, their performance improves (Earley & Perry, 1987).

Pre-Goal Setting Reflection Questions

- [ ] Why is this goal important?

- [ ] What do I want to accomplish?

- [ ] What priorities do I need to change in my life to make this happen?

- [ ] What exactly are we going to do, with or for whom?

- [ ] What strategies will be used?

- [ ] What advice should I collect before setting this goal?

- [ ] What impact will this goal have on my life and work?

- [ ] What are my desired results?

- [ ] What resources do I have?

- [ ] Who else needs to be involved?

- [ ] Who is going to do what?

- [ ] How am I going to do this?

- [ ] How can this goal be measured?

- [ ] How will I know if I have reached my goal?

- [ ] What is this goal going to cost?

☐ When do I want this to be completed?

☐ How much time do I have?

☐ Is the timeframe achievable?

☐ Has anyone else done this successfully?

☐ Is the objective described with action verbs?

☐ Is it clear what needs to happen?

☐ Is it clear where this will happen?

☐ Is the outcome clear?

☐ Is this possible?

☐ Is it possible to achieve this objective?

☐ Is the "why I am doing this" well understood?

☐ Do I understand the limitations and constraints?

10 Things That Will Help Me Achieve My Goals

1   Keep a daily record of your time.

2   Set goals that motivate you.

3   Consolidate activities into blocks of time.

4   Find a like-minded tribe.

5   Concentrate on priorities

6   Delegate what you can.

7   Set a strict daily plan & follow it!

8   Daily check what you plan to do versus what you actually did.

9   Allocate your time in relation to your goals.

10   Take corrective action as needed.

Goal Setting
2 Types of Goal Setting

Professional Goal Setting

Furthering Your Education

Professional Development

Licensing or Certification

Job Promotion

Team Goal Setting

Can Include Team Goal Setting

Personal Goal Setting

Health Goals

Financial Goals

Family Goals

Professional Goal Setting

Defined your goal:

What does research say about your goal?

Failure Factors:

Strategies:

Team Goal Setting

Defined:

What does research say about professional goals setting?

Failure Factors:

No team vision or buy-in:

Stages of Performing:

Lack of data:

No consensus:

Strategies:

Rewards:

Positional power, Verbal praise, Recognition in front of peers

Personal Goal Setting

Defined your goal:

What does research say about your goal?

Failure Factors:

Strategies:

Lack of support:

Personality:

Emotional Factors:

Social Factors:

Economic Factors:

Goal Setting Considerations

☐ Frequency

☐ Strategies & Tips

☐ Annual Goals Setting

☐ BOY (Beginning of the Year)

☐ MOY (Middle of the Year)

☐ EOY (End of the Year)

More Research Based Goal Setting Recommendations

- Theory and research suggest a shortlist of ways to use goal setting effectively as a component of self-regulation. The following strategies are especially useful (Schunk, D. H., 2001).

- Subdivide a long-term goal into proximal sub-goals. Help learners determine what sub-goals must be accomplished to attain their long-term goals.

- View the goals as reasonable and commit to attaining them. Provide verbal encouragement (e.g., "You can do this.") to motivate learners to accomplish their goals.

- Self-monitor progress. Students must learn how to gauge progress in learning or performance. Provide progress feedback on tasks where it is difficult for learners to gauge progress independently.

- Use strategies for coping with difficulties. When progress is minimal, students might seek help, attempt to determine a more effective strategy or re-evaluate the goal and timelines.

- Self-evaluate capabilities. The perception of progress will strengthen self-efficacy, which is critical for continued motivation and self-regulation.

CONCLUSION

Goal setting is an integral component of self-regulation. Setting goals is a generic strategy that can be applied in various domains. Effective goal setting requires people to set a long-term goal, break it into short-term, attainable sub-goals, monitor progress, assess capabilities, adjust the strategy and goal as needed, and set a new goal when the present one is attained. This multi-step plan is key to promoting healthier human functioning, higher motivation and perceived self-efficacy, and self-regulated learning and performance across the life span (Schunk, 2001).

Goal Strategies

1. Set SMARTER Goals

Anyone serious about achieving his or her goals needs to understand the importance of the SMARTER goal-setting method. The SMARTER acronym stands for specific, measurable, achievable, relevant, time-bound, evaluated, and re-adjusted goals. It is a strategy for setting your goals, resulting in a high probability of success.

To set a SMARTER goal, you need to get highly specific about that goal. Describe it down to the very last detail, ensuring that it is measurable and achievable. While lofty long-term goals are okay, SMARTER one-year goals, should be something that is slightly out of reach but still attainable.

Relevant means the goal must be in harmony with your values and beliefs and in tune with who you are deep down inside. Time-bound simply means that you have assigned a specific calendar date to its achievement. In addition, as you work toward the goal, you must evaluate and adjust your plan to achieve it.

2. Create a Plan of Action

Planning is one of the most important strategies associated with achieving any goal. Yet, many fail to create detailed and intricate plans to realize our dreams. Instead, we have some abstract notion in our minds that will only get us part of the way there, but it will not help bring those goals to fruition.

Anyone serious about a goals needs to create a massive action plan and must be willing to take action daily— every day without fail—to reach their heart's desires. So make a plan and obsess over it, working on it tirelessly, day and night, until you reach your goals.

3. Eliminate Bad Habits

Clearly, bad habits can hold us back from achieving our goals. They stifle our progress and get in the way of our hopes and our dreams. Anyone intent on achieving anything worthwhile knows that they need to stamp out the bad habits that hold them back.

While eliminating bad habits is difficult, you can overcome them if you find a stronger reason than the habit itself. Of course, it does not happen quickly or painlessly. It happens slowly, over time. However, by eliminating your bad habits, you can easily illuminate a pathway for eventually reaching your goals.

4. Instill Self-Discipline

Self-discipline allows us to put our goal achievement on cruise control. To the disciplined person, anything is possible. To the person who lacks self-discipline, any menial task can seem too daunting. The surest road to becoming a self-disciplined person is through your habits.

By instilling the proper habits into your life, you can become self-disciplined. Habits such as waking up early, practicing gratitude, eating healthy, exercising, and getting ample sleep help instill that much-needed self-discipline into our lives. With the right set of habits in your life, anything is possible.

5. Lessen Your Distractions

Distractions interrupt our progress, yet the world is full of distractions.

The most common distraction comes from technology that offer an intimate connection to the world's. Considering that smartphones and social media have upended industries and commerce and how we interact with one another, it's no wonder it's become harder and harder to stay productive during the day.

You have to learn to cancel out the noise. First, consciously become aware of the distractions around you, then work to cut them off. This is certainly one strategy for achieving your goals. Turn off the phone, the internet, and the television, and slip into a world where you're purely focused on the task ahead.

Related: 5 Big Distractions That Sabotage Your Entrepreneurial Success

6. Leverage Daily Goal Setting

Daily goals are a great way to stay focused and on track toward your long-term goals that are years and years away. It is easy to lose sight of those big goals when struggling with a moment-to-moment challenge to avoid drowning in our own responsibilities. However, those daily goals provide markers that are easier to stick to and focus on.

This strategy calls for setting goals every single morning without fail. What will you accomplish and achieve today? Take your month-long or 12-month goals and break them down into milestones. Whatever it is, as long as it is measurable and you break it down into what you need to achieve that day, it is easier to stay on track.

7. Avoid Procrastination

Procrastination is the silent killer that keeps us from achieving our goals. It stifles our progress and forces us to retreat into the clutches of comfort and habit. Everyone knows that to achieve anything worthwhile, you must stamp out procrastination. Take action rather than wait another day or moment to do what should be done now.

One strategy for taking action and avoiding procrastination is to use the 15-minute rule. Set a timer on your smartphone for 15 minutes and commit to doing the one thing you have been putting off for the longest. Only for 15 minutes— no longer. The commitment is too small to fail, and once you do take some action, you have just created a bit of momentum. You might just keep going after that.

8. Manage Your Time.

One strategy for achieving anything in life is to become an effective manager of your time. Those who can best manage their time can achieve the loftiest goals. To do this, you need to institute an effective system for managing the precious little time you have rather than squandering it away. You can break up your day into four sections and plan tasks.

9. Chase the Frog

Mark Twain once said, "If it's your job to eat a frog, it's best to do it first thing in the morning. And if it's your job to eat two frogs, it's best to eat the biggest one first." He was referring to the big-ticket items on your to-do list, the ones that would provide the most benefit toward your long-term goals. We also call these our MITs, or the day's _most important tasks_.

In this strategy, you're chasing the frog by tackling your MITs first thing in the morning. Be sure to take on those big Quadrant 2 tasks at the start of the day to get them out of the way. While you might not see immediate results from your actions, it does add up over time. Do it nice and early when you're freshly rested.

10. Implement the Pareto Principle

The Pareto Principle, also known as the 80/20-Rule, states that 80 percent of the results come from 20 percent of the efforts. In sales, this also means that 80 percent of the sales come from 20 percent of the customers. However, this dives even further to show that, within the 20 percent producing 80 percent of the results, 20 percent of that subset also produces 80 percent of the results.

The point? Focus your attention on scaling out the small set of efforts producing the biggest results. To engage in this strategy, you first need to identify which efforts are actually achieving the biggest gains. But, once you do, all you need to do is scale out those efforts.

11. Welcome Failure

While some might not think this is a strategy for achieving anything, failure is by far one of the surest pathways to success in any endeavor. And some of the world's most famous people have failed many times. The difference between them and the next person is that they didn't give up.

Learn to welcome failure when it comes knocking on your door. Accept it. Understand it. Learn from it. Then move past it. Leverage your failures as learning experiences so that you can start fresh and do it again. Henry Ford once said, "Failure is simply the opportunity to begin again; this time more intelligently."

12. Seek Out Daily Doses of Inspiration.

While we might all want to achieve something monumental in life, as much as we try to stick it out and see things through, we often get discouraged. As soon as that happens, the negative-thinking gears begin turning, and the what-if doomsday scenarios begin playing out in our minds.

Fear becomes that stalker in the night, ready to suffocate and stop us off from achieving our goals. To counteract that, seek daily doses of inspiration. Reach out to others who have achieved the success you are going after. Listen to their stories and get inside their heads. What was it like for them to endure failure after failure? How did they bounce back and achieve their goals?

13. Find a Mentor

Navigating the turbulent seas of commerce and business can be catastrophic at best. We do not always know the right direction to sail in. In addition, often, our ship can take on water and sink when we don't know the next steps to take to stay afloat. Finding a mentor can help you survive and reach the shores of hope.

Mentors help shine a light, illuminating a pathway toward success. Like a beacon in the night, shining brightly through the misty fog, they help us reach our goals.

14. Set up a system for tracking.

If you are serious about achieving anything, you need to track your progress. You can evaluate and adjust your progress to reach your goals when you track. When you don't track, you have no clue where you are, how far you've come, or just how much you have left to go.

If your goals are measurable, then they are trackable. Track them every single day. Similar to how a plane would chart and track its progress from moment to moment, you need to track your own progress to ensure that what you are doing is working. Without meticulously tracking your goals, you are wasting your time.

15. Welcome Criticism

People are often critical of others, especially when they see them experience a bit of success. They try to chop you down, and when you do fail, they're there to call you out on it, telling you that you should have never tried to achieve that lofty goal in the first place.

You should welcome that criticism. Don't run from it. Listen to what they have to say and allow it to fuel you to achieve your goals rather than to hold you back. We all fail. The more we fail, the more chances we have to succeed. If you want something bad enough, it should not matter what anyone says about it. Use it to drive and push you forward rather than hold you back.

10 Types of Data Walls for Life and Work

What are data walls?

Data walls are designated walls or bulletin boards that display important information. _Confidential information cannot be disclosed, such as birthdays or identification numbers._ Below are ten types of wall displays you can consider displaying data, recognition, and motivational quotes for others in life and work. When we show things on a wall, we say loud and proud, "This is important to me." If you look around, you can know a lot about a person. You can see their families, religious quotes, or college degrees. What are you showing others?

Data Walls For Life:

☐ Displaying your dreams and goals.

☐ Displaying personal progress on a wall is a constant reminder and a great way to keep you on track.

☐ If you are trying to get out of debt or pay off bills, what you owe and have paid will curve your spending.

☐ Display a project you are working on.

☐ Display family goals or progress.

Data Walls For Work:

☐ Displaying percentages of attendance or project completion is a great way to display data. This keeps everyone in the know.

☐ Display customer feedback.

☐ Display organizational growth or projects.

☐ Celebrate small wins.

☐ Display quarterly reports.

12 Self-Reflection Questions for the Career of Your Dreams

1   How do you want your life to be?

2   What are all your choices?

3   What can move you towards the career of your dreams?

4   What are self-limiting beliefs about yourself?

5   What beliefs do you need to know to achieve the life of your dreams?

6   What would you do if time, money, and experience were not a concern?

7   What would you do or learn if you knew you couldn't fail?

8   What is stopping you from moving forward and achieving your goals?

9   What are the ten most important work values to you?

10   What will you commit to knowing to move forward?

11   What are you passionate and energized by?

12   What are your current skills, abilities, and talents?

Chapter 3
Employee Engagement

"Research indicates that workers have three prime needs: Interesting work, recognition for doing a good job, and being let in on things that are going on in the company."

-Zig Ziglar

Let's start with these two questions!

What is employee engagement?

Why is employee engagement important?

The Pancake Story

Once, there was a young intern, bright-eyed and excited about making a difference in the world and within his organization. The intern was smart, likable, and eager to learn. His priority was to build relationships with the people he managed. He was thrilled to get started and make a difference in his new position. He arrived at the office on his first day of work in his new role. "Hi, I am your new manager," he said. However, the new manager was quickly sat down and told: (1) Do what I say, not what I do, (2) don't rock the boat, and (3) If it's not broken, don't fix it.

Inside, his stomach and heart hurt. This was not what he expected. This was not what he studied in school. He thought, "What did I do wrong?" All his textbook dreams of leading and creating change toward a common goal crumbled underneath him. A tsunami consumed everything he learned from his mentors. What do you do when working with someone who has no desire to have a professional relationship with you? How do you work with a transactional leader who will never be pleased no matter what you do?

The intern was humble, self-motivated, and worked with whatever his boss dished out. Some days it affected him, and some days it did not. But the biggest twist to this story was everyone else loved the big boss. At first, he could not understand why. The big boss was cold, unimpressionable, and moody. Why did everyone love the big boss? Why did everyone have a professional relationship with the boss except him? Was it personal? Maybe the boss just hated the intern. Maybe there wasn't trust; after all, he was new? The poor intern struggled to understand what lay beneath the iceberg. There were days the intern was okay and made copies and sharpened pencils as he was told to do. His thoughts were, "I'm getting paid pretty well, so I'm just going to do what the big boss tells me to do." And some days, he did not want to get out of bed and hated his job, his life, and thought he needed to get out of there. "My boss hates me, and I can't take this anymore." The big boss limited the intern's responsibilities. The intern felt like an overpaid secretary.

What should the intern do next?

A   Quit!

B   Go to Human Resources and ask for a transfer even though he has only been there a few weeks.

C   Reach out to a mentor.

D   Keep trying to win the respect of the big boss.

E   Call in a few political favors and try to get the big boss fired.

Continued:

The intern got along with the other coworkers. He saw a lot of need for improvement. There were many ways he thought he could make the organization even better. Everything was like a roller coaster. Some days were good, but some days were bad, depending on the big boss's mood. The intern reached out to an older mentor who had been there and done that. They met for coffee on a Saturday, and the intern explained his situation. His mentor chuckled. That was not the reaction the intern had expected. "Why are you laughing?" the intern questioned the mentor. The mentor advised him to give it a year. "A year?"

Why did the mentor say to give it a year?

A The mentor is empathetic.

B The mentor thinks a lot can happen in the year, and the big boss might have a change of heart.

C The mentor doesn't want the intern's resume to look like he was jumping around and couldn't handle the job.

D The mentor thinks that the intern is not finished learning from the situation yet.

Continued:

The mentor explained that every situation is a learning situation. "Learn what to do and learn what not to do when you are the big boss." This is all preparing you. That Monday, the big boss was preparing for a big meeting and gave the intern a bunch of meticulous tasks to complete before the meeting, including running more copies. Out of frustration, the intern opened his mouth and said, "Aren't the employees supposed to be doing these things? Why am I doing it for them?" The big boss looked at the intern, taken back. "You have a lot to learn, intern," the big boss said with a sneer. The intern thought, *Oh, great. Now the big boss is really going to hate me.* The big boss handed the intern a list of tasks to complete for the employees, a grocery list, and fifty dollars. The intern thought, *now I am a personal assistant.* However, the intern had a hefty mortgage, so he did what the big boss said and even tried to smile. The intern filled the copy machine with paper, left the copy machine running, and went to the grocery store as fast as possible to purchase all the things on the list the big boss had given him.

What should the intern do next?

A   Quit!

B   Try to understand the big boss's rationale.

C   Ask the big boss a bunch of questions.

D   Go back to the office, take the initiative, and set everything up.

E   Go back to the office, ask the boss for direction, and stay out of trouble.

Continued:

The intern returned to the office with a bunch of grocery bags, and the big boss was waiting for him with his arms crossed. As luck would have it, the copier jammed, and there was paper everywhere. Big boss shot the intern a look with eyes that could kill. "You're supposed to be leading this organization, and you left the copier running, and it jammed." What could the intern say? "I'm sorry, I just wanted to get everything done for you as fast as I could. I know this meeting is important to you."

"Set up the conference room. I'll be there in a few minutes," the big boss ordered. The intern cleared the copier, got the copies running again, and took the groceries to the conference room. He brought the copies, set them on the table, and took all the groceries out of the bags. A few minutes later, the big boss walked in with a large box of pastries and cookies and a beautiful white tablecloth hanging over his arm. The intern attended to the big boss quickly and helped with the tablecloth. The big boss said to take everything out of the box, put it on that table, and make sure everything looked nice for the employees. "I'll be back." The big boss came back with a griddle, an apron, a chef's hat, and a bunch of door prizes. The intern was very confused. The big boss plugged in the griddle and set it to low. Upon the table were plates, forks, napkins, butter, and syrup, all set up nice and neatly. The big boss looked at the intern and said, "Make sure the coffees hot and start pouring the juice into cups."

The intern was still confused but continued to work on the coffee and juice, and the employees started trickling in one at a time with smiling faces. They went straight to the big boss, hugged and kissed him, and told him how wonderful he was. "Big boss, you make the best pancakes."

"That's the least I can do for all your hard work. I appreciate everything you do, and I try to make sure you know how much you are appreciated."

The intern could not believe what he was hearing and seeing. He stood back, smiled, shook hands, and passed out the juice. The Big boss smiled and continued to flip pancakes. He asked the employees questions about their families and projects they were working on. Everyone was engaged and happy to see one another.

What should happen next?

A The intern should confront the big boss. After all, why wasn't he treated the same?

B Let it go and not say anything?

C Ask all the employees why they love the big boss, and tell them how badly he is treated?

D Call Human Resources and ask for a mediation?

E File a grievance?

What are 3 things you learned?

1 _____

_____

2 _____

_____

3 _____

_____

Engagement Activities for Life and Work

1   Let someone go ahead of you in traffic.

2   Assign a buddy/mentor for every newcomer.

3   Learn to say hello in a new language and practice with others.

   Get a cart and pass out water, bananas, and apples to co-workers.

4   Reconnect with someone with whom you have lost contact.

5   Celebrate people.

6   Write a letter or an email to someone who impacted you this week.

7   BBQ.

8   Say "yes" the next time someone asks you for help.

9   Celebrate your wins and goals.

10   Leave a positive comment on a website or blog.

11   Have themed office days.

12   Show them the "people" results of their work.

13   Have a meeting outside on a beautiful day.

14   Be the first to forgive.

15   Create an open sharing space where employees can work together.

16   Create excitement about upcoming opportunities.

17   Consider more flexible work hours.

18 Say something positive when you see someone who needs it.

19 Make a bird feeder and put it somewhere your family or co-workers can see it.

20 Tell someone how much you appreciate them.

21 Create a team mascot.

22 Pass out popsicles.

23 Let someone go ahead of you in line.

24 Book study.

25 Write a handwritten note to recognize exceptional work.

26 Make sure new hires get to know the whole team.

27 Give your boss recognition for his/her hard work.

28 Eat outside with coworkers and enjoy the day

29 Buy your co-worker lunch.

30 Leave coupons in the lunchroom.

31 Send out some Monday motivation.

32 Find out about someone else's culture.

33 Be the first to say, "I'm sorry."

34 Support a local shop or business.

35 Start a newsletter.

36 Encourage personal projects.

37 Give directions to someone who is lost.

38 Smile and say hello to five strangers today.

39 Donate blood.

40 Hold the door open for someone who has his or her hands full.

41 Offer healthier options at your workplace

42 Let someone else have your prime parking space.

43 Designate "Super Hero T-shirt Day."

44 Organize employee games, tournaments, and competitions.

45 Emphasize work-life balance.

46 Make a welcome sign for someone who has come home or back to work.

47 Say something nice about someone in public.

48 Set up an organizational library where coworkers can trade and donate books.

49 Take time to say thank you to a parent, child, or co-worker.

50 Identify people who make work engaging.

51 Take the time to fill out a survey that compliments.

52 Organize a toy drive and donate them to a local school, hospital or shelter.

53 Send out an employee survey to get honest feedback.

54 Encourage and provide learning opportunities.

55 When you finish a good book, leave it for someone else.

56 The next time you are tempted to complain, find something positive to say.

57 Buy the next person in line a coffee.

58 Tidy up a public/office space.

59 Spend time with other employees.

60 Ban emails for a day

61 Bring a birthday card for a co-worker.

My Aha Moments

My Passions

My Mentors

My Mentees

_____

My Visions

My Inspiration

My Project

My Community

My Ideas

My Creativity

My Spirit

My Memories

My Team Members

My BIG Dreams

My Positive Energy

My Loved Ones

My Priorities

My Research

Also Written by Christina DeMara

Igniting Leadership

50 Research-Based Strategies for Life & Work

Peace Is Mine

The Forgiveness Journal

I'm Not Broken

The Power of Prayer, Scripture, and

Interactive Journaling

I Will Not Fall

The Power of Prayer, Scripture, and

Interactive Journaling

How God Saved Me

My Mother's Memoirs on Abuse, Depression

& Overeating

How God Healed Me

My Mother's Memoirs on Grace, Health, Gastric Bypass & Reconstruc-
tive Surgery

The I Am Journal

A Soul-Searching Journal for Creative Women of God

Isaiah 43:2

40 Days of Scriptures, Reflection, and

Journaling for the Lent Season

Meaningful Books & Resources

Meaningful Leadership

How to Build Indestructible Relationships with Your

Team Members through Intentionality and Faith

Meaningful Leadership Journal

Meaningful Leadership Prayer Journal

Meaningful Teacher Leadership

Reflection, Refinement, and Student Achievement

Meaningful Writing & Self-Publishing

Your Guide to Igniting Your Pen, Faith, Creativity & Entrepreneurship

Early Life Leadership Books & Resources

Early Life Leadership Research

Where Do Leaders Come From?

Early Life Leadership in Children

101 Strategies to Grow Great Leaders

Early Life Leadership

101 Conversation Starters and Writing Prompts

Early Life Leadership Workbook

101 Strategies to Grow Great Leaders

Early Life Leadership Workbook for Girls

101 Strategies to Grow Great Leaders

Early Life Leadership Kids Journal

Early Life Leadership in the Classroom

Resources, Strategies & Tidbits to Grow Great Leaders

About the Author

Christina DeMara is the idealistic creator and author of the two leadership doctrines coined as Meaningful Leadership and Early Life Leadership. Above that, she is a Christian, mother, wife, educator, public speaker, curriculum creative, and promoter of kindness. Her first job as a high school dropout was at fifteen, working for the Kirby Vacuum Company. She later completed her bachelor's degree in Interdisciplinary Studies with a minor in Special Education, where she found a deep passion for teaching students with exceptionalities.

She proudly holds three master's degrees in Special Education, Educational Administration, and Leadership, and a third in Curriculum and Instruction from the University of Texas-Rio Grande Valley. She has experienced and studied leadership theory, organizational models, and business strategy. She is best known for her creative idea formulation and interactive books: Early Life Leadership Workbook for Girls, and I'm Not Broken: The Power of Prayer, Scripture, and Interactive Journaling. Christina DeMara has overcome many obstacles in life through the grace of God and tries every day to inspire others. She enjoys spending time with her family, going to the beach, church, cooking, research, teaching, do-it-yourself projects, and trying new restaurants.

Please Connect with Christina!

She would love to hear from you!

Christina has two Facebook groups called

I Love Reading & Writing

and

I Love Leadership

for her readers.

You are welcome to join!

Bless This Book!

If you enjoyed this book or any other of Christina's books, your honest review is greatly appreciated!

Reviews help others see the author's books and help the writer qualify for different book promotions.

Your Time and Review is Always Appreciated!

Questions?

ChristinaDeMara.com

christinademara@gmail.com

References

Allen, T. D., Eby, L. T., Poteet, M. L., Lentz, E., & Lima, L. (2004). Career benefits associated with mentoring for protégés: A meta-analysis. Journal of Applied Psychology, 89(1), 127.

Back, A. L., Arnold, R. M., Baile, W. F., Tulsky, J. A., & Fryer☒Edwards, K. (2005). Approaching difficult communication tasks in oncology 1. CA: A Cancer Journal for Clinicians, 55(3), 164-177.

Bandura, A. (1997). Self-efficacy: The exercise of control. New York: Freeman.

Barnard, R. A., Cruice, M. N., & Playford, E. D. (2010). Strategies used in the pursuit of achievability during goal setting in rehabilitation. Qualitative Health Research, 20(2), 239-250.

Boekaerts, M., Pintrich, P. R., & Zeidner, M. (Eds.) (2000). Handbook of self-regulation. San Diego: Academic Press.

Davis, B. D., & Muir, C. (2004). Learning soft skills at work: An interview with Annalee Luhman. Business Communication Quarterly, 67(1), 95-101.

Dweck, C. S. (1999). Self-theories: Their role in motivation, personality, and development. Philadelphia: Taylor & Francis.

Eby, L. T., Durley, J. R., Evans, S. C., & Ragins, B. R. (2006). The relationship between short-term mentoring benefits and long-term mentor outcomes. Journal of Vocational Behavior, 69(3), 424-444.

Erez, M., & Earley, P. C. (1987). Comparative analysis of goal-setting strategies across cultures. Journal of Applied Psychology, 72(4), 658.

Gould, D. (1986). Goal setting for peak performance. Applied Sport Psychology, 133-148.

Latham, G. P., Mitchell, T. R., & Dossett, D. L. (1978). Importance of participative goal setting and anticipated rewards on goal difficulty and job performance. Journal of Applied Psychology, 63(2), 163.

Latham, G. P., Mitchell, T. R., & Dossett, D. L. (1978). Importance of participative goal setting and anticipated rewards on goal difficulty and job performance. Journal of Applied Psychology, 63(2), 163.

Locke, E. A., & Latham, G. P. (2002). Building a practically useful theory of goal setting and task motivation: A 35-year odyssey. American Psychologist, 57(9), 705.

Locke, E. A., & Latham, G. P. (1990). A theory of goal setting and task performance. Englewood Cliffs, NJ: Prentice Hall.

Locke, E., & Latham, G. (1994). Goal-setting theory. Organizational Behavior 1: Essential Theories of Motivation and Leadership, 159-183.
Locke, E. A., Shaw, K. N., Saari, L. M., & Latham, G. P. (1981). Goal setting and task performance: 1969–1980. Psychological Bulletin, 90(1), 125.

Meyer, E. C., Sellers, D. E., Browning, D. M., McGuffie, K., Solomon, M. Z., & Truog, R. D. (2009). Difficult conversations: improving communication skills and relational abilities in health care. Pediatric Critical Care Medicine, 10(3), 352-359.

Rekha, K. N., & Ganesh, M. P. (2012). Do mentors learn by mentoring others? International Journal of Mentoring and Coaching in Education, 1(3), 205-217.

Robles, M. M. (2012). Executive perceptions of the top 10 soft skills needed in today's workplace. Business Communication Quarterly, 75(4), 453-465.

Schunk, D. H. (2001). Self-regulation through goal setting. ERIC Clearinghouse on Counseling and Student Service, University of North Carolina at Greensboro.

Schunk, D. H. (1995). Self-efficacy and education and instruction. In J. E. Maddux (Ed.), Self-efficacy, adaptation, and adjustment: Theory, research, and application (pp. 281-303). New York: Plenum Press.

Schunk, D. H., & Zimmerman, B. J. (1997). Social origins of self-regulatory competence. Educational Psychologist, 32, 195-208.

Smith, L. S., McAllister, L. E., & Crawford, C. S. (2001). Mentoring benefits and issues for public health nurses. Public Health Nursing, 18(2), 101-107.

https://www.dol.gov/odep/topics/youth/softskills/softskills.pdf, 2019

WebsterDictionary.com

Zaccaro, S. J., Rittman, A. L., & Marks, M. A. (2001). Team leadership. The Leadership Quarterly, 12(4), 451-483.

Zimmerman, B. J. (1998). Developing self-fulfilling cycles of academic regulation: An analysis of exemplary instructional models. In D. H. Schunk & B. J. Zimmerman (Eds.), Self-regulated learning: From teaching to self-reflective practice (pp. 1-19). New York: Guilford Press.

Zimmerman, B. J. (2000). Attaining self-regulation: A social cognitive perspective. In M. Boekaerts, P. R. Pintrich, & M. Zeidner (Eds.), Handbook of self-regulation (pp. 13-39). San Diego: Academic Press.

www.ingramcontent.com/pod-product-compliance
Lightning Source LLC
Chambersburg PA
CBHW071837200326
41519CB00016B/4140